All About Vaccines

A Reader For Children And Parents

Written and Illustrated
By
Bridget Gongol

A special thank you to
the family, friends, and medical professionals
who graciously edited this book with me.

Your help, patience, expertise,
and guidance are greatly appreciated.
I couldn't have done this without you.

Hey there!

Do you want to learn more about vaccines?
Well, you are in the right place. You might have
questions about vaccines like:

What are vaccines?
How do they work?
Why are they important?

In this book we are going to talk about the answers
to these questions. As soon as you are ready,
turn the page and read on!

Vaccines are an amazing scientific invention.
They are very important because they protect us
from diseases and even save lives.

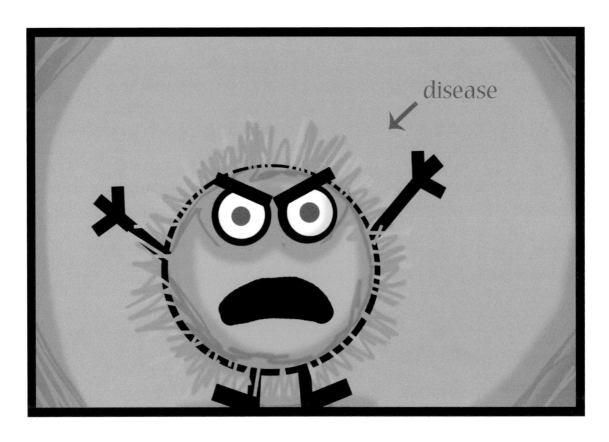

So, how do vaccines work?
Well, a vaccine is made from a disease.
It might be made from a part of a disease,
or a weakened or dead form of a disease.

That form of a disease in a vaccine is
injected into your body. This means it gets
put into your body with a shot.

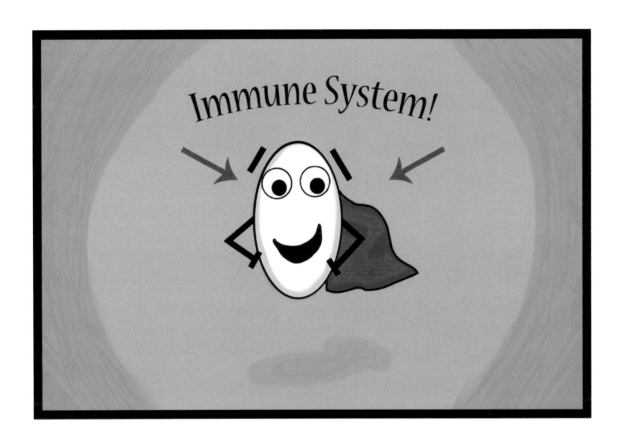

When a vaccine is injected into your body,
your immune system goes to work.
Your immune system is like a superhero
that protects you from getting sick.

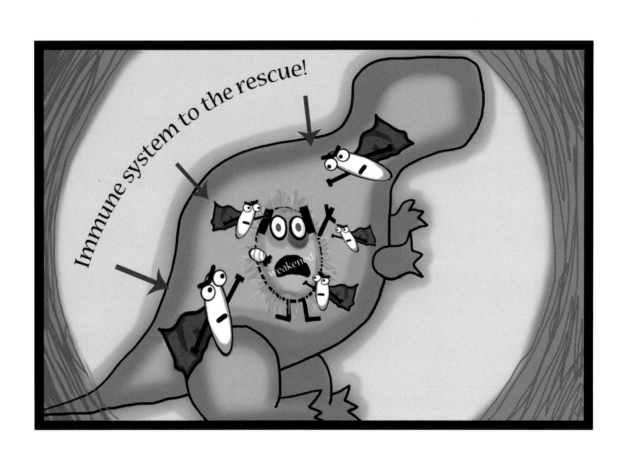

After a vaccine enters your body, your immune system learns how to fight and destroy the disease in a vaccine. When this happens, your body becomes immunized from the disease.

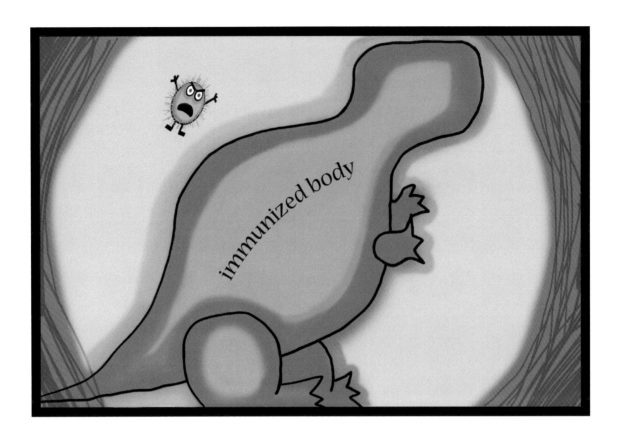

Being immunized means that if a disease tries to
make you sick after you get vaccinated,
your body can protect itself from the disease.

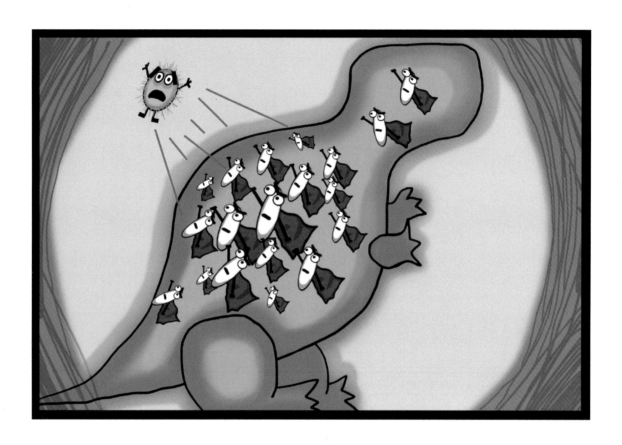

Instead of getting sick, your body's immune system
already recognizes the disease and knows
how to fight and kill it. It's pretty awesome.

When you get your vaccines,
a doctor or a nurse will give you a shot.
It will probably hurt – but only for a little bit.

When it's over, you will be protected
from all sorts of scary diseases!

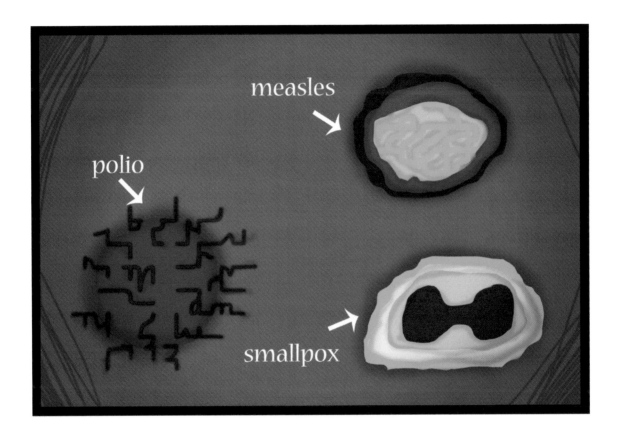

Because they protect us from diseases, vaccines are really important. Before we had vaccines, a lot of people got very sick from illnesses like polio, measles, and smallpox. With vaccines, we don't have to worry about getting sick from these diseases anymore.

It's also really important that you get
vaccines because there are some people who
are too little or too sick to get vaccinated.
When you get your vaccines, you protect yourself
and the people who can't get vaccines, too.

This is because when you get your vaccines,
you act like an immune system for the people who
can't get vaccines. If everyone who can get vaccines
is vaccinated, diseases can't live or make anyone sick.
This helps to protect everyone from diseases.

We know all of these things about vaccines
because of science – and science is amazing!
There are many, many scientists and doctors who
work on vaccines to make sure they are safe.

So stay healthy! Protect yourself and your loved ones
by getting those vaccines!

If you have questions, please be sure to ask your
doctor or nurse. Thanks for reading!

The End*

*...but only of this book.
Certainly not the end of science.

All About Vaccines
for parents and older children:
more information!

Like we talked about earlier, vaccines are very important because they protect us from diseases. After vaccination, if your body actually encounters a disease (like measles, mumps, whooping cough, or any of the other 20+ vaccine-preventable diseases) your body can defend itself against the potential infection. Instead of getting sick, your body's immune system already recognizes the disease and knows how to destroy it.

Sometimes people don't like to trust vaccines because they think they are "new", but in reality, the concept behind vaccination is nothing new or scary. It's been around for a long time. Variolation (a practice similar to vaccination where people were exposed to weakened forms of diseases as a means of developing immunity) was widely practiced as early as the 1700s.

Before vaccines were developed to fight them, diseases like polio ravaged populations. Due to recent efforts to eradicate this disease (through vaccination), the number of cases of polio dropped from 350,000 cases in 1988 to just 187 cases in 2012 worldwide. Due to similar worldwide efforts to vaccinate against measles, the number of deaths from measles dropped 71% between the years 2000-2011. Because of vaccines, we no longer have to worry about paralysis from polio, death from measles, or any of the other debilitating effects from vaccine-preventable diseases.

It isn't mere coincidence that the occurrence of diseases like polio, mumps, whooping cough, and measles dropped dramatically with the onset of widespread immunization practices.

In fact, if vaccinations were stopped, each year about 2.7 million deaths could be expected worldwide from measles alone. To put this into perspective, this is the equivalent of wiping out an entire city the size of Chicago in one fell swoop - every year.

It's true that vaccinations can carry some risks, but most of the scarier risks happen so rarely that an actual correlation between vaccinations and these risks is hard to determine. This means if you have a negative reaction to a vaccine, it's possible that you were a one in a million case that had a complication from a vaccine, or perhaps you were just a one in a million case of having a complication from some unknown event that happened to occur at the same time you were vaccinated.

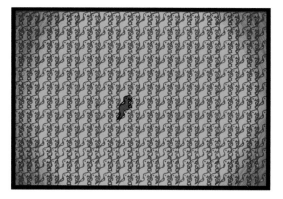

The vast majority of people experience either very mild or no side effects after receiving vaccines. Most people just take a mild pain reliever after their injections. It's also important to remember that most vaccines take around two weeks to reach full efficacy, so if you are exposed to a disease you could still get sick during this time.

A common concern is that there is some correlation between vaccinations and autism. This is simply not true. Vaccines don't cause autism. The only report that claimed a link between autism and vaccines was proven to be fraudulent, and the person in charge of that false report had his medical license revoked for his dishonest work. Other claims against vaccines concerning the preservatives in vaccines are unfounded as well. International studies have been conducted between countries that do and do not use thimerosal (the antiseptic preservative in question) and the consensus is that it is not harmful in the low doses present in vaccines. Rates of autism are the same in countries that do and do not use thimerosal in their vaccines. Regardless, most childhood vaccines don't even contain thimerosal anymore, and emerging evidence suggests that autism actually begins long before birth. It's a non-issue.

Another common misled belief is that children receive too many vaccines when they are too young and that this overwhelms their immune system. This is also untrue. Children are exposed to an incredible number of pathogens every day – far more than are present in any vaccine or group of vaccines that are commonly given at the same time. Vaccines are given to children in the amount they are and at the rate they are in order to build their immune systems quickly. This helps to protect children from as many diseases as possible as soon as is possible.

What is most important to know is that the risks posed by actually contracting vaccine-preventable diseases are far greater than any possible risks associated with any vaccine. Not getting immunized puts you at risk of getting sick from preventable diseases that can put your life at risk. What's more, if you don't get immunized, you are not only putting your own life in danger, but you are also compromising herd immunity, which in turn puts everyone at risk of contracting these diseases.

So, what is "herd immunity"? In any group, there exist a certain number of people who can't receive immunizations for legitimate medical reasons. (For example: infants, pregnant women, or those who are otherwise immunocompromised like cancer patients.) When an individual can't be immunized themselves, they rely on herd immunity to protect them.

Herd immunity means that those who are immunocompromised and can't get vaccinated are protected from disease. This protection stems from the fact that everyone around them (the herd) is immunized. If the herd can't get infected, then those who can't be immunized can't get infected, either.

If you don't get immunized by choice, this puts you at risk of infection. When you get needlessly infected, you put those who can't be immunized at risk, too. Diseases get passed from person to person, and the herd gets infected. This can (and does) lead to totally unnecessary deaths.

Science is amazing. Modern medicine makes life better, but only if we respect it. We can trust the medical community on the effectiveness and importance of vaccines because we can see the effects through history. More importantly, this information is peer-reviewed. This means that experts in the medical field read and criticize work and research on vaccines repeatedly in an attempt to get at the most accurate information.

When scientific sources like the Centers for Disease Control and Prevention, the World Health Organization, and the National Library of Medicine release research, it has been fact-checked multiple times by numerous experts. When they say things like, "get vaccinated" it isn't just because one person thought it was a good idea; it's because many experts and mounds of data confirm it.

In sum, vaccines are an amazing scientific achievement. They prevent illnesses, and in doing so, save lives. Protect yourself, your loved ones, and those around you by staying fully vaccinated.

Hopefully this book has answered some of the questions you may have about vaccines. For more information, be sure to talk to your doctor and check out websites like the Centers for Disease Control and Prevention (www.cdc.gov), the World Health Organization (www.who.int), and the National Library of Medicine (www.nlm.nih.gov).

Thanks for reading!

Vocabulary Index

Booster Shot - A vaccine shot given to children and adults to maintain immunity against a disease. Vaccines sometimes wear off over time so it's important to get booster shots to ensure that immunity to diseases is still active.

Chickenpox - See *Varicella*

Contagious Disease - A disease that is easily spread from person to person. It can be spread by human contact, contact with an infected object, or through the air.

Diphtheria - A contagious disease caused by bacteria. Symptoms include fever, weakness, sore throat, and swollen glands. A thick coating can build up in the throat or nose, making breathing very difficult. Complications include airway blockage, heart damage, nerve damage, paralysis, and lung infection. With treatment, 1 in 10 infected people will die. Without treatment, 1 in 2 infected people will die. This disease can be prevented with the DTaP vaccine.

Epidemic - A widespread outbreak of a disease in a population.

German Measles - See *Rubella*

Haemophilus Influenza - Bacteria that can cause several different diseases including ear infections, pneumonia, blood stream infections, meningitis, skin infections, inflammation of the windpipe, and infectious arthritis. Symptoms vary by disease, but may include fever, cough, chills, muscle pain, headache, tiredness, vomiting, diarrhea, light sensitivity, and confusion. Complications vary by disease but may include brain damage, hearing loss, loss of limbs, and death. These bacteria and the diseases they cause can be prevented with the Hib vaccine.

Hepatitis A - A liver disease that results from infection from the Hepatitis A virus. Symptoms include fever, nausea, vomiting, abdominal pain, joint pain, and jaundice. Complications include liver failure and in extreme cases, death. This disease can be prevented with the HepA vaccine.

Vocabulary Index, Continued

Hepatitis B - A liver disease resulting from infection from the Hepatitis B virus. Symptoms include fever, nausea, vomiting, abdominal pain, joint pain, and jaundice. Infected people can develop chronic disease, which can result in liver cirrhosis and liver cancer. This disease can be prevented with the HepB vaccine.

Herd Immunity - The concept that if enough of a population is immunized against a disease, the whole community is protected from the disease. For some diseases, a vaccination rate of 90-95% of all individuals in the population is needed to maintain herd immunity. When a population dips below this threshold, the population is at risk of an epidemic outbreak of a disease.

Immune System - A complex network of cells, organs, proteins, and cell-forming tissues that protect the body from disease and other foreign substances.

Infectious Disease - A disease typically caused by germs that is spread by contact with an infected person.

Measles - A highly contagious disease caused by a virus that is spread through the air. Symptoms include fever, rash, runny nose, and cough. Of the children infected with this disease, 1 in 10 will get an ear infection, 1 in 20 will get pneumonia, 1 in 1,000 will get encephalitis, and 1-2 in every 1,000 will die. In pregnant women who get infected, it can cause early delivery or even miscarriage. This disease can be prevented with the MMR vaccine.

Meningitis - A disease caused by meningococcal infection. Symptoms include stiffness, fever, nausea, vomiting, light sensitivity, and confusion. Complications include hearing loss, brain damage, and death. This disease can be prevented with the Meningococcal vaccine.

Mumps - A contagious disease spread through the mumps virus. Symptoms include fever, headache, muscle ache, tiredness, loss of appetite, and swelling of salivary glands. Complications can include swelling of the testicles, ovaries, and breasts, encephalitis, meningitis, and deafness. This disease can be prevented with the MMR vaccine.

Vocabulary Index, Continued

Peer Review - When experts within a field read, criticize, and correct the work of others in the same field (their peers) to ensure that the best information is provided to the public. This also ensures that several people agree on a new idea, preventing one person from pushing an unfounded idea or concept.

Pertussis - A respiratory illness caused by bacteria, usually spread by coughing or sneezing. Symptoms include runny nose, fever, apnea (a pause in breathing), and most noticeably, fits of coughing so severe that they result in vomiting and exhaustion. Of the children infected with Pertussis, ½ of them will be hospitalized. Of those hospitalized, 1 in 4 will get pneumonia, 1-2 in 100 will suffer convulsions, 2 out of 3 will have apnea, 1 in 300 will suffer disease of the brain, and 1-2 in 100 will die. This disease can be prevented with the DTaP vaccine.

Pneumonia - See *Streptococcus Pneumoniae*

Polio - A highly infectious disease caused by a virus. Symptoms include fever, fatigue, stiffness in the neck and back, nausea, and pain in the limbs. Complications include paralysis of the limbs and paralysis of the respiratory system (breathing system), which can lead to permanent disability and even death. This disease can be prevented with the IPV vaccine.

Rotavirus - A contagious disease caused by a virus. Symptoms include fever, watery diarrhea, vomiting, and stomach pain. Complications include dehydration and death. Rotavirus causes more than 500,000 deaths each year among children under 5 years old worldwide. This disease can be prevented with the RV vaccine.

Rubella - A contagious disease caused by a virus. Symptoms include rash and low-grade fever. Complications include birth defects if contracted by a pregnant woman such as deafness, mental retardation, cataracts, heart defects, liver damage, and spleen damage. This disease can be prevented with the MMR vaccine.

Vocabulary Index, Continued

Smallpox - A serious contagious disease that is caused by a virus. Symptoms include fever, headaches, body aches, and a rash that covers the body and tongue in red spots. This rash eventually becomes pus-filled blisters that scab and cause scarring. Complications include scarring, blindness, and death. This disease has been eradicated (eliminated) due to worldwide vaccination efforts.

Streptococcus Pneumoniae - Bacteria that can cause many illnesses, including pneumonia, ear infections, meningitis, sinus infections, and blood stream infections. Symptoms vary by disease, but may include fever, chills, cough, difficulty breathing, headache, and confusion. Complications vary by disease but may include hearing loss, developmental delay, and death. These bacteria and the diseases they cause can be prevented with the PCV vaccine.

TB - See *Tuberculosis*

Tetanus - An infection caused by bacteria. Symptoms include headache, jaw cramping, muscle spasms, painful muscle stiffness all over the body, trouble swallowing, fever, and seizures. Complications include bone breaking, lung blockage, pneumonia, breathing difficulty, and possible death due to breathing problems. This disease can be prevented with the DTaP vaccine.

Tuberculosis - A disease spread through the air that is caused by bacteria. Symptoms include cough, coughing blood, chest pain, fatigue, weight loss, fever, and chills. Complications include joint destruction, meningitis, impaired liver function, and death. Tuberculosis is a leading killer of those infected with HIV. This disease can be prevented with the BCG vaccine.

Varicella - A very contagious disease caused by a virus. Symptoms include fever, tiredness, and an itchy rash that covers the body. Complications include dehydration, pneumonia, inflammation of the brain, bacterial infections of the skin, blood stream infections, bone infections, joint infections, and death. This disease can be prevented with the Varicella vaccine.

Whooping Cough - See *Pertussis*

Sources

Briggs, Helen. "Autism 'begins long before birth'." BBC News. 26 Mar. 2014. BBC. 27 Mar. 2014.
‹http://www.bbc.com/news/health-26750786›.

DeStefano, Frank, Cristofer S. Price, and Eric S. Weintraub. "Increasing Exposure to Antibody-Stimulating Proteins and Polysaccharides in Vaccines Is Not Associated with Risk of Autism." The Journal of Pediatrics. 01 Apr. 2013. The Journal of Pediatrics. 28 Mar. 2014.
‹http%3A%2F%2Fwww.jpeds.com%2Farticle%2FS0022-3476(13)00144-3%2Ffulltext›.

"Frequently Asked Questions about Immunisation." Immunise Australia Program. Australian Government Department of Health. 28 Mar. 2014.
‹http://www.immunise.health.gov.au/internet/immunise/publishing.nsf/Content/faq#6›.

"Frequently Asked Questions about Multiple Vaccinations and the Immune System." Centers for Disease Control and Prevention. Centers for Disease Control and Prevention, 07 Dec. 2012. Web. 22 Apr. 2014.
‹http://www.cdc.gov/vaccinesafety/Vaccines/multiplevaccines.html›.

"Frequently Asked Questions About Thimerosal (Ethylmercury)." Centers for Disease Control and Prevention. Centers for Disease Control and Prevention, 14 Oct. 2011. Web. 22 Apr. 2014.
‹http://www.cdc.gov/vaccinesafety/Concerns/Thimerosal/thimerosal_faqs.html›.

"History and Epidemiology of Global Smallpox Eradication." Centers for Disease Control and Prevention. Centers for Disease Control and Prevention. Web. 22 Apr. 2014.
‹http://emergency.cdc.gov/agent/smallpox/training/overview/pdf/eradicationhistory.pdf›.

"How Vaccines Prevent Diseases." Centers for Disease Control and Prevention. 08 Mar. 2012. Centers for Disease Control and Prevention. 15 Mar. 2014.
‹http://www.cdc.gov/vaccines/parents/vaccine-decision/prevent-diseases.html›.

"Immunization and Vaccine-Preventable Disease." Immunization and Vaccine-Preventable Disease. Stanislaus County Public Health Services. 17 Mar. 2014.
‹http://www.schsa.org/PublicHealth/pages/immunization/html/diseases.html›.

"Measles." WHO. Feb. 2014. World Health Organization. 15 Mar. 2014.
‹http://www.who.int/mediacentre/factsheets/fs286/en/›.

"NCIRS-National Centre for Immunisation Research and Surveillance." MMR Decision Aid. 2009. National Centre for Immunisation Research and Surveillance. 16 Mar. 2014.
‹http://www.ncirs.edu.au/immunisation/education/mmr-decision/measles.php›.

Sources, Continued

Park, Alice. "Great Science Frauds: Andrew Wakefield." Time.com. 12 Jan. 2012. Time Magazine. 12 Feb. 2014.
‹http://healthland.time.com/2012/01/13/great-scienpce-frauds/slide/andrew-wakefield/›.

"Polio." Definition. 11 Mar. 2014. Mayo Clinic. 17 Mar. 2014.
‹http://www.mayoclinic.org/diseases-conditions/polio/basics/definition/CON-20030957›.

"Possible Side-Effects From Vaccines." Centers for Disease Control and Prevention. 04 Feb. 2014. Centers for Disease Control and Prevention. 16 Mar. 2014.
‹http://www.cdc.gov/vaccines/vac-gen/side-effects.htm›.

"Vaccines Not Associated With Risk Of Autism." Centers for Disease Control and Prevention. 29 Mar. 2013. Centers for Disease Control and Prevention. 16 Mar. 2014.
‹http://www.cdc.gov/vaccinesafety/Concerns/Autism/antigens.html›.

"What Would Happen If We Stopped Vaccinations?" Centers for Disease Control and Prevention. 18 Sept. 2013. Centers for Disease Control and Prevention. 16 Mar. 2014.
‹http://www.cdc.gov/vaccines/vac-gen/whatifstop.htm›.

About the Author:

Bridget Gongol is an artist and teacher who loves science, languages, and animals.
She spent many hours when she was younger preparing for her book career by writing
and illustrating books with her brothers for their "library", which still proudly resides in
her parents' home in Iowa.

For more of her work, please visit www.bridgetgongol.com

Logan Hocking County
District Library
230 E. Main St.
Logan, OH 43138

CPSIA information can be obtained at www.ICGtesting.com
Printed in the USA
LVIW01n2009250717
542598LV00010B/210